101

Ways to Be Smart About
Money

Rebecca Vickers

Chicago, Illinois

Edited by Andrew Farrow and Adam Miller
Designed by Richard Parker
Picture research by Ruth Blair
Originated by Capstone Global Library, Ltd.

Library of Congress Cataloging-in-Publication Data
Vickers, Rebecca.
  101 ways to be smart about money / Rebecca Vickers.
    p. cm.—(101)
  Includes bibliographical references and index.
  ISBN 978-1-4109-4382-8
  1. Finance, Personal—Juvenile literature. 2.
Thriftiness—Juvenile literature. 3. Money—Juvenile
literature. I. Title. II. Title: One hundred one ways to
be smart about money. III. Title: One hundred and one
ways to be smart about money.
  HG179.V55 2011
  332.024—dc22   2010033913

Photo Credits
Alamy: Ei Katsumata, 43, TAO Images Limited,
24; Getty Images: AleksandarNakic, 32, cjp, 9,
grandriver, 20 right, Jamie Grill, 14, jentakespictures,
41, keeweeboy, 15, MsLightBox, 29, ooyoo, cover,
WEKWEK, 20 left; Nora Coon: 6; Shutterstock:
Alexander Kalina, 7, Andresr Trendy, 4,
CandyBoxPhoto, 28, Chavdar, 48, Clara, 21, cozyta,
36, Denis Pepin, 31, Greg Perkins, 47, haveseen,
35, Nemida, 19, Nousha, 5, PhotoSky 4t com, 50,
Prometheus72, 13, pryzmat, 45, Robyn Mackenzie,
22, Thinglass, 23, Valentyn Volkov, 18, Wire_man, 37,
Worytko Pawel, 34, Yuri Arcurs, 27, 39

Table of Contents

In order to protect the privacy of individuals featured in case studies, some names have been changed.

Words appearing in the text in bold, **like this**, are explained in the Glossary.

Are You Money Smart?

Money is a big part of your life. It is great to get a chance to earn your own money and decide how you want to use it. By being money smart, you can benefit from your hard work, while also getting good value from your spending and saving. Go for it!

Many things that you want will cost you money. Just make sure you get good value for your cash.

01 Put all your loose change into a jar or bowl. Don't lose it in the wash, down the back of couches, or in the back of drawers. You will find that the jar soon fills and adds up!

02 When you go shopping, make a list of the things you really need. That way you are less likely to spend money on things you don't need.

03 Think twice before ordering soft drinks in restaurants. The cost is high for what you get. Remember, tap water is free.

04 When you are planning to get something expensive, such as an MP3 player, don't rush into buying the first one you like. Do some online research to check and compare prices. You will be surprised by how much you might save.

Quiz

Are you a money dummy?

1) You are given money for your birthday. You:
   a. use it as part of your usual spending money
   b. go out and buy an item that you have wanted for a long time
   c. put it in a savings account

2) When you go out for the day, you:
   a. take all the cash you have with you in case you need it
   b. think about what you are planning to do and take enough money to cover your needs
   c. take no cash so you don't buy things you don't need

3) It's safer to put your money in your pocket than to keep it in a purse or bag.
   a. true
   b. false
   c. both can be risky

Each coin may be worth very little, but together it all adds up.

Nora Coon: writing her way to success

When she was only 12 years old, schoolgirl Nora Coon pitched an idea for a book to a publisher's representative at a writing convention. By the time she was 17, three of her nonfiction books for teens had been published. And by 22, she was an established writer. How did she make this happen?

Nora knew that her talents were storytelling and writing, and decided early to make her dream of being a writer come true. Her second book, *Teen Dream Jobs*, was written to help other teens find the careers they want. Nora has not let her diabetes and epilepsy hold her back. In fact, one of her books, *The Diabetes Game*, focuses on young people with this disease. Nora has made her talents, knowledge, and personal experiences really work for her.

Nora Coon didn't let anything stop her fulfilling her dreams.

"All teenagers are stupid about money. It's just a phase you have to go through."

Do you agree with this 15-year-old's opinion? Do you think Ephren Taylor would agree?

Don't despair! There are many ways to go about earning some spending money.

Aim for the top!

05 Good ideas and money-making plans can come to you at any age. Be confident, and your ideas could lead to great things!

06 Remember, your own talents and experiences are key to your financial success. Being smart about how you use your money is as important as how you make it.

07 If there are things you want but cannot afford, consider making them yourself.

08 If fears and excuses are holding you back in life, then be brave and move forward with things!

09 Make firm money plans and stick to them. This is the start of being money smart.

It All Adds Up

The fact is you cannot save or spend money if you don't have any! So, how do you get ahold of some cash? You usually start by getting pocket money from your parents, possibly for household chores you do, and as presents for birthdays and holidays.

Negotiating your pocket money

In the adult world, salary negotiations can be difficult and complicated. Coming to an agreement with your parents over your pocket money can be just as difficult! If you keep in mind the following tips, you will have a firm and fair base to start your bargaining.

10 Figure out which of your expenses your pocket money will cover. Will it include school lunches and clothes, or will it also pay for things such as school trips and extra activities? Make a list of all the household chores that you are expected to do in order to get your pocket money.

11 Do you feel you need extra pocket money to deal with rising costs or unexpected additional expenses? Write out a clear list of these to show your parents. But remember, if your parents say a firm NO, you need to accept that the negotiations are over.

12 Your negotiations will be more successful if you can be trusted to be sensible. If you are careless or stupid with your money, you cannot expect your parents to be sympathetic to requests for more.

BE SMART

Everyone's different
Remember that the work schedules and finances of every family are different. A fair agreement with your parents might not be anything like the arrangements your friends have.

If you do a really good job cleaning someone's car, that person may ask you to do it again or recommend you to others.

> **"I made my allowance as a kid cleaning toilets. I'm actually pretty good at it."**
>
> —Jennifer Aniston, actor

Earning money

The pocket money you get from your parents will never seem like quite enough! So, what do you do?

There are lots of ways you can earn money by helping others out—for example, by babysitting, washing cars, or mowing lawns. You also need to think about how much time you have and if you will need to spend any money for equipment. Relatives, friends, and neighbors can be good customers. However, if you are looking for more customers than that, you will need to advertise yourself.

So, how do I market "me"?

If you want customers other than your relatives and friends, there are ways to market yourself without spending big money. Simple, clear information is all that is needed.

13 Make your own business cards on a computer by printing your details onto thin cardboard and cutting them out. A business card should give your name, contact details, and clearly state the work you can do. A memorable or interesting business name, such as "Matt and His Mower," can give you an edge over the competition.

14 Use a computer to design a flyer or poster to advertise your services. There are bulletin boards in many places that let you put up small posters for free or for a small charge. It won't cost you anything except a bit of your time to hand-deliver posters and flyers to houses in your neighborhood.

15 When you have done a job for someone, ask if that person would be willing to recommend you to others. A personal recommendation from a satisfied customer is the best free advertising.

16 The most important tip for anyone running a business, even if it is just mowing grass or babysitting, is that THE CUSTOMER IS ALWAYS RIGHT. The customers are paying you, so if they don't want their kids to watch television, or want their grass clippings put into garbage bags, as long as it is legal, give them what they want.

A bit of work and imagination on your part can help attract customers.

Happy Dogs

Pet Care and **Walking Service**

Local recommendations available

Jenny Kendall
barkingmad97@zedmail.com

The world of work

As you get older, you and your friends will eventually get part-time, weekend, or summer jobs. Remember: You ARE protected! Most countries have rules about the age you have to be before you can work, the maximum numbers of hours you can work in a week, and the minimum amount of pay per hour that you can earn. So when the time is right, just how do you get the job?

17 Think about the kind of place you would like to work. It is true that most people eventually get part-time jobs in stores and restaurants, but why not try something different? If you have always wanted to work with animals, ask your local veterinarian or pet shop if they have any part-time or weekend work.

18 Prepare a simple **résumé** to give out. If you want to get a good job that pays well, you need to present yourself well. You will stand out from other applicants if you have a well-organized résumé with all your contact details.

What's that?
A *résumé* is a brief report of a person's education and work experience, and sometimes certain biographical details. It lets potential employers get to know you and your experience in a quick glance.

Q What is **financial literacy**?

A Literacy is the ability to read and understand written words. In the same way, financial literacy means having an understanding of money and making good decisions about how to save and spend it.

When you apply for any kind of job, remember that *you* are the product you are trying to sell. To get the money, you need to get the job!

19 First impressions count! When you go for a job interview, remember how important it is to look clean, neat, and appropriately dressed.

20 When you inquire about a job on the phone, the way you sound can influence your success. Speak clearly, politely, and give sensible answers. It may make the difference between getting a job or not.

21 Practice makes perfect. Think of the kinds of questions you might be asked on the phone or in an interview, and practice your responses beforehand.

22 When you get a job, the same behavior that helped you to get it can make you a good employee *and* make you extra money. For example, if you are a waiter in a restaurant, being polite, helpful, and efficient can get you bigger tips from your customers.

Oops!
Find out about the law! There are protective employment laws to keep young people safe and stop them from being taken advantage of.

23 Don't accept any job from an employer who tries to pay you less than the minimum wage. This is the lowest amount of money by law that you can be paid per hour to do a job.

24 Never accept a job that requires you to accept "cash only." This probably means your employment is not official, and is therefore illegal.

25 Don't do anything you know to be dangerous or perform tasks without the correct clothing or equipment. No amount of money is worth the risk of injuring yourself.

true story

The teenager who sold records from the trunk of his car

Today, Richard Branson and the Virgin company name are well-known all over the world. But his life as an international **entrepreneur** really started at the age of 16, when he produced a magazine for students.

At the age of 19, he was selling reduced-price vinyl record singles from the trunk of his car, and then by mail order. Within only three years of starting his first businesses, he had record stores in central London and a recording studio. Over 40 years later, he is now a billionaire. Branson is still enlarging his business empire and using some of his wealth to indulge his adventurous spirit. He has attempted to break records in fast boats and hot-air balloons.

Cash for junk

Everyone ends up with things they don't want and don't need. You grow out of clothes, and your likes and dislikes can change, too. All that extra stuff takes up space—and it can be worth money! So how can you make some cash and get that embarrassing old bike out of the garage?

26 Make sure that everything you want to sell is clean, workable, and well-presented. Wash, iron, and fold clothes and put similar sizes or types of items together. Clean up old toys and make sure all the parts of games and puzzles are in the bag or box. Make each thing look like it is worth buying.

27 Collect all the stuff you want to sell and have a garage sale.

28 Keep an eye open for local flea markets, but remember that you will need transportation and may have to pay a fee to take part.

29 Find local stores that let you display small postcard ads. These may be free or cost a small weekly rate.

30 Look through the local newspapers, including any free papers. There are usually sections for small "for sale" ads.

31 Identify potential customers. If you have outgrown your bike, would your friend's younger sister like it?

Even when you no longer want something, someone out there will be willing to pay you for it.

Often the best thing to do with stuff you don't need or want is to give it away to friends, relatives, or to a charity store. Or you could have a sale for a charity. People are usually generous when buying things at a charity sale, and the cash you make can go to your chosen good cause.

If you sell an item that is jointly owned, don't forget to share the cash.

32 Be sure that an item is yours to sell! If your parents bought you an expensive bike, you need to ask if they are okay with you selling it, or whether they want some of the money you make. If it is something that once belonged to a grandparent, it is probably not yours to sell. You might find in years to come that you are very glad you kept it!

33 When an item is jointly owned by the family, such as a swing set, you need to agree how the money will be split before you sell it.

34 If you are selling items from an ad that gives your home phone number, check first that this is okay with your family. Then make sure that they have all of the details about the item in case you are not there when potential buyers call.

35 NEVER let anyone come to your home to pay for or pick up an item unless there are adults in the house. Have the item ready by the door, and only accept payment in cash.

When the Piggybank Is Full...

So, your piggybank is bursting with all the money you have saved up. Where should you keep it? You could opt for a shoebox under the bed. Or you could take the leap and enter the real money world of banks and **credit unions**.

But is this as scary and difficult to understand as it first seems? Even more importantly, is your money really safe once you no longer have it in your hands?

listen up!

The media are full of phrases such as "credit crunch," "recession," and "low **interest** rates." It can seem really scary out there! But starting a bank or credit union account is still a good idea for four main reasons:

1. Putting your money in a bank account protects it from theft, loss, or damage.
2. A bank account helps you to develop a **credit history**. If you stick to the rules, you may be able to borrow money from the bank in the future, for a **mortgage** or a business loan.
3. A bank account can get you into the habit of saving.
4. Money in savings accounts can earn you interest.

What's that?

Interest is the amount of money you get paid by a bank or credit union on savings, or that you get charged on borrowings or debt. The interest rate is the percentage paid or charged.

Good bank? Bad bank?

It is worth spending time choosing a bank or credit union that will give you the best services and interest rates.

36 Do your research before choosing a bank. Make sure whichever one you choose has the right account or accounts for you. Check if there are special accounts for young people or students.

37 Try to choose a bank that does not charge fees for transactions or services provided. These charges can quickly add up.

38 Choose a bank that is convenient to get to. If the nearest branch is far away, maybe it's not for you.

39 Make sure that the bank is part of a company insured by the national government. This means that any money you have in your bank account will be safe even if the bank runs into trouble.

Oops! Don't be tricked by special offers or gifts that are trying to encourage you to open an account in a particular bank or credit union. Always judge a bank on bank-related matters, such as interest rates and other services.

Is interest interesting?

Most banks and credit unions offer a choice of different kinds of accounts. Savings accounts pay you interest to keep money in the account, rather than spend it. The amount of interest you get is based on a percentage of the amount saved. The interest is then added to the savings. This is called compounding. Look for savings accounts that give a good rate of interest and compound the interest often.

Bank cards: Understanding plastic

Credit cards, debit cards, personal identification numbers... When you get a bank account, you need to learn a whole new language! You also need new knowledge and new habits.

What's the difference between a credit card and a debit card?

A credit card lets you buy items and then pay at the end of the month. It is called a credit card because the company is giving you credit to buy the items.

A debit card is issued with your bank account and is used to get cash from automatic teller machines (ATMs) or to pay for items in stores. It takes money directly out of your bank account as you use it. You have to have the money in order to spend it!

Debit cards use PIN technology. This means you have to enter your personal identification number (PIN) before the payment will go through.

In addition to credit and debit cards, you can also get prepaid credit cards. These cards work like prepaid cell phones. You pay to have credit put on the card, and then it can be used to buy things. These can be useful when you don't want to carry cash, or when want to buy items on the Internet or by mail order without having to give your bank details.

Oops!

Amanda thought it would be easier to remember her PIN number if she used her birth date, December 10—or 1210. Then she had her purse stolen from her bag in a restaurant. It contained her driving license, which showed her date of birth.

By the time she had reported the theft, her card had been used at an ATM with the correct PIN! What had seemed an easy way for her to remember her PIN was also an easy guess for the thief. Choose a friend's birthday to make it more difficult!

Protect your information by always using one hand to cover the other when entering your PIN at an ATM.

Don't throw your money around!

Cash and cards are valuable possessions. Treating them properly is an important part of being money smart.

40 Never carry more cash than you need. It can make you a target for theft and tempt you to spend more than you should.

41 Keep your cards safe! Find a secure place at home to keep debit or credit cards. If cards get stolen or lost, call the phone number relating to loss or theft on your bill or bank statement. Your card will then be deactivated, so it cannot be used.

42 Never take your cards or excess cash to school. You won't need these things during the day, and they could get lost or stolen.

43 When you go out, keep cards and cash secure in your purse or wallet and carefully replace them after use.

44 Handbags containing valuables such as cash, cards, and cell phones should be zipped up or securely fastened. Keep wallets in deep, preferably front pants pockets.

45 Try not to put wallets or purses in the outside pockets of your backpack. They will be safer shoved to the bottom of the largest section with other things on top.

listen up!

It can sometimes be difficult to find a secure place to keep cash or cards. This may especially be the case when you are traveling.

Experienced travelers know that hidden money belts work best. These can go around your waist and under your clothes like a belt, or around your neck inside your shirt, or they can be clipped to a bra.

Oops!

When you have just used an ATM to withdraw cash, try not to get distracted by your friends or the line behind you. Make sure you take both your card and your cash, and put them safely away BEFORE you turn around. Make life more difficult for pickpockets and purse-snatchers!

BE SMART

It's best to keep valuable items in your front pockets. But in crowded places like concerts, someone may even try to reach into these. You can close up front pockets using large safety pins, or by sewing Velcro fastenings inside the top edges of your pockets. Or you could wear clothes with deep pockets that zip or button up.

46 In an emergency, some folded paper money can go in your shoe under your foot until you need it. It may get smelly, but it will definitely be safe!

47 For days at the beach, you can buy small, watertight containers for your money and valuables. You can wear one on a neck cord or fastened to your wrist or bathing suit.

Oops!

Money and plastic cards are not indestructible. Try to keep them safe and take good care of them. If accidents do happen, here are some ways to sort things out:

48 Oops! Your paper money has accidentally gone through the washing machine! If you are lucky, you will just end up with really clean money. If you are unlucky, you end up with money mush. Let it dry out thoroughly and then take it to a bank. If over half of the bill is there, you will probably be able to get a replacement.

49 If money is ripped or torn up, you can tape it together and still use it. However, banks will replace damaged money as long as the serial numbers on both halves match.

50 When credit cards and debit cards get scraped, bent, or cracked, or their magnetic strips get demagnetized, they may not work in ATMs or PIN machines. You will need to contact your card provider and apply for a replacement card.

Australian dollars are made of an almost indestructible plastic material. The bills stay clean, are hard to **counterfeit**, and are recyclable!

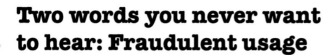
Two words you never want to hear: Fraudulent usage

Kamal was a bit shocked when his bank statement showed that he had bought over $50 of gasoline at three different places in the same week. Since Kamal isn't old enough to drive and doesn't have a car, he knew that something was very wrong!

Kamal immediately called the bank's customer service number on the back of his statement. He found out that he had been the victim of **fraudulent usage** and it was probable that his debit card had been **cloned**. It took nearly a month for the bank to credit the illegally obtained money back to his account. But it could have been worse. What if he hadn't checked his bank statement?

Always check your bank statements to make sure the amounts of money going in and out of your account are correct.

Is It Safe to Spend?

Once you have earned money and set up your banking account, what about a little spending? You deserve it! But remember, even though it is okay to spend, it isn't okay to go crazy. You need to think about the difference between needing something and wanting it, as well as about being a savvy saver.

Earning and saving your own money gives you the chance to get some of those special items you want. If you do this, you don't need to wait for birthday money or depend on the Bank of Mom and Dad!

Budgeting: Keeping track of that cash

Before you can spend, you need to know how much money you have. The only way you can do that is to always keep track of your cash. In addition to checking your bank statements, it is a good idea to do a simple budget. A budget sets out what you think you will spend over a weekly or monthly period. When making a budget, there are a few things to remember:

51 Always be realistic when setting your budget. If you always spend a certain amount for lunch at school, don't presume you can suddenly start spending half that amount.

52 A good budget should NEVER include more outgoing money (expenditures) than money available to spend. A budget should always balance—money in and money out should be the same. Aim to have something left after the period covered by your budget.

53 Money you add to your savings should be one of the "expenditures" in your budget.

You can be your own **accountant**, and your budget can be as simple or complicated as you want.

DATE	IN	OUT
December 25	$100 (Xmas money)	
January 1	$80 (January allowance)	
January 5		$65 (tickets for concert)
January 12	$12 (car cleaning)	
January 19	$15 (babysitting)	
January 20		$27 (school stuff)
January 23		$48 (shirt + shoes + DVD)
January 27		$8 (birthday present for Tom)
TOTAL FOR MONTH	$207	$148

listen up!

Make sure that when you buy something it is because you really want it, not because you have been influenced by advertising or marketing.

54 Just because something is marketed using well-known celebrities, that doesn't mean it is better—only that the company has a large advertising budget! A great jingle or catchphrase may be fun, but it doesn't make a shampoo or a deodorant more effective. Look on the Internet or in specialized magazines for product reviews to get the real story of what is good and what is not.

55 Beware of the use of "placement" advertising. Companies make sure that items they want to sell to teenagers are advertised during television programs aimed at young people. This just means that the advertisers are smart, not that the product is the best you can get.

Don't let the logo bullies get you!

Now that you know how to really look at a product and not just at who is doing the advertising, you also need to be sure that companies aren't pressuring you to part with your money in other ways.

 Q What is a **logo**?

 A A logo is a symbol used by a company to identify a product as belonging to its brand. It is usually a small shape, word, or series of letters. Only buy brand name goods if they are the best you can get for the price, not in the hope that a logo will impress someone else.

56 Don't let friends convince you that you can *only* be cool if you buy products of a specific brand. **Peer pressure** should not be the reasoning behind how you spend your money. Base your spending choices on quality and cost, not on conforming to someone else's ideas.

57 Always comparison shop before you buy. This means checking the price on the same or similar items to see where you can get the best deal.

58 Shopping when there are special sales may bag you bargains, but never use sales as an excuse for **impulse buying**.

listen up!

The first thing to understand when budgeting is the difference between *wanting* and *needing*. You may want to download some music or get a new pair of cool boots, but do you really need them? The answer isn't always no! A pair of great boots can still fulfill a need if they don't cost more than they should. Also, one reason for earning and saving money is so you can sometimes afford to get things you want, even if you don't really need them.

Making the most of your money

When you are going shopping, there are many ways you can make your hard-earned cash stretch.

59 Always take advantage of store loyalty cards or preferred customer points programs. They can save you money in the long run.

60 Collecting coupons is not just for your grandma! There are often coupons in newspapers, magazines, or online that will give discounts or two-for-one deals.

Buying sale items at the end of a season can make your money go much further.

61 Check the labels on clothes, or the packaging of products, to see where the item is made. You can then research the work practices in that country to see if they are fair to workers.

62 Do some Internet research for information about the **ethical** work practices of stores and brands. Their websites might have a section explaining how the company tries to be ethical or "green."

Make sure the things you buy have been produced ethically and are not damaging the environment.

Q When is a bargain not a bargain?

A When retailers aren't quite telling the whole truth! Trading and advertising standards (laws) prevent retailers from telling outright lies. However, they can still be very sneaky....

- A sale item in one store may not really have been more expensive there, but only at another store in the chain.
- Stores will advertise items at very cheap sale prices, but there are actually only very small numbers available. They hope that customers will come to get those products and then spend their money on other things when they can't get what they want.
- Another trick is the use of a "loss leader." This is when a heavily discounted item is promoted to tempt you into the store in the hope you will also buy full-priced items.

Beware! Store credit cards are *not* the same as store loyalty cards. Store credit cards are run by stores and can be used only to buy products in that store or at others in the same chain. Using store credit cards can lead to debt, so avoid them unless there are real benefits.

When you spend your money on a hamburger or a roast beef sandwich, you don't imagine that you are contributing to the destruction of the rain forest—but you might be! For example, the need for cattle-grazing land to meet the demands of the beef market has been a major cause of South American rain forest destruction.

listen up!

63 Look for special logos that identify products as ethically produced or environmentally sound. These include Fairtrade, Organic Cotton, Rainforest Alliance, and many others.

64 Think about the **carbon footprint** of a product. Is there something made more locally that would be just as good?

What's that?

A **carbon footprint** means the total amount of greenhouse gases emitted by an activity or the making of a product. Your carbon footprint is made up of all of the greenhouse-gas-creating activities that you cause over a given period of time.

case study

Watch out for "not included"!

Erin went to buy a new printer at a large computer discount store. She'd done some research and thought she had found the best deal. Luckily, just before she got to the front of the checkout line to pay, she noticed, "Ink cartridges not included" written on the box. With the extra cost of the cartridges, it turned out that another printer that included cartridges in the price was actually much cheaper.

Oops!

Most people know about the addictive power of alcohol and drugs, but did you know that shopping can be addictive, too? When people do something they enjoy, it causes the release of substances called endorphins into the bloodstream. Endorphins reinforce the enjoyment. Some people need to feel that pleasure again and again. Others become shopping addicts because of low self-esteem. Shopping addiction can be as difficult to break as an alcohol or drug habit.

Q Are the symptoms of a shopping addiction just high spending?

A No. A true shopping addict buys things he or she doesn't need, or buys ridiculous numbers of the same item. Most items never get used and are hidden away, or even destroyed. Buying stuff gives shopping addicts some temporary relief from the negative feelings they have about life, but it can lead to shame, remorse, and guilt.

true story

Celebrity spending gone mad!

Katie Holmes, Mike Tyson, and Britney Spears have all hit the headlines with their spending habits. But the celebrity who has really caught media attention is former child star Lindsay Lohan. She has been reported to have spent up to $15,000 a week on shopping sprees, and $7,000 a month on her hair!

Fun for (Almost) Free

Yes—you really can have fun and do interesting things without breaking the bank! New is nice, but new-to-you is almost as good! Swapping things with friends or buying things from secondhand or charity stores can help you keep your money in your pocket, or in the bank.

Old clothes or fabric from a garage sale can be snipped and sewed into something unique for very little money.

listen up!

Group money-saving and money-earning activities can be fun *and* economical.

65 Get together with a group of friends and choose a swap party theme—for example, clothes, DVDs, CDs, video games, or books.

66 Arrange a "trash into cash" sale of unwanted goods with a group of friends. You can divide the money up or pool it together for a group outing or treat.

67 If you and your friends need new outfits for a special event, make a group decision to get everything you need secondhand or from charity stores. See who can spend the least on great things.

Kate Moss and thrift store chic

Many high-profile celebrities get their super-cool, stylish looks by wearing secondhand clothes. Model Kate Moss has often been spotted going through thrift stores for some of the individual outfits that keep her at the forefront of fashion. Since becoming a part-time clothes designer, Kate admits that many of the pieces in her latest collection are based on used items she bought from thrift stores in the United Kingdom and the United States.

listen up!

It's all in the words. If you say "secondhand" or "used" clothes, it sounds...well, tacky! If you say "retro" or "vintage fashion," suddenly it's very cool.

Here are some things to bear in mind when buying secondhand:

68 To get the best value out of secondhand items, avoid overworn, damaged, or stained clothing.

69 Buy items for their individual parts. For example, great buttons can be cut off a not-so-great shirt and used on something else.

70 Thrift stores and charity stores are great places to get accessories. Look out for funky and original belts, ties, and bags.

71 Look in different sections of charity stores for original gifts, or for interesting and quirky things to personalize your room.

Short of money? Make it yourself!

Another way to plug the gap in your limited finances is to make things you might want or need, either for yourself or as presents for your family and friends. It's personal, thoughtful, and cheap!

72 Think twice before spending money on manufactured greetings cards. Some are ridiculously expensive for what they are. Instead, attach a small paper label to a gift, or tap into your creativity and make the card yourself!

73 Think creatively (and economically) when wrapping gifts. Newspaper tied up with colorful strips of fabric can look great. Or try using leftover pieces of old wallpaper or leftover bits of fabric.

74 Family and friends always appreciate gifts of food. Something tasty and homemade always wins out over store-bought goods.

75 Consider offering vouchers for your services as gifts. These could be for lawn mowing, cleaning, babysitting, or many other things. Make sure it is something you are really good at, such as painting fingernails or solving computer problems.

If you receive a personal, handmade gift,
you have something that is one of a kind.

> **"One of the best presents I ever had was an amazing piece of art my cousin made out of junk.... It made my room look like a cool art gallery."**
>
> —Dave, age 15

More flash than cash

Do you want to have fun with your friends, but no one can afford to spend the cash? Why not try some do-it-yourself fun! Keeping your money in your pocket doesn't need to be boring.

76 Have a DVD theme night at someone's house. Make a list of all the movies you already have on a particular theme—such as horror or science fiction—then vote for the two you want to watch. If everyone chips in for snacks, the cost will be minimal.

77 If the weather is good, explore the great outdoors! A picnic with a Frisbee, even if it's just in a local park, can be a nearly free day out.

78 Be a little geeky and have a Scrabble or other board game competition. You know you will enjoy it, especially if someone makes crazy winner and runners-up certificates to hand out at the end.

79 Video arcades eat money! Make a list of all the games you and your friends have, and create a lending system.

Fun with friends does not mean spending lots of cash.

Stuff can get ruined

One of the simplest ways to be money smart is to take good care of the possessions you value. Failing to do this is wasting money you have already spent. If you keep your stuff in good condition, you have the option of selling things for good prices when you don't want them anymore.

80 Never put drinks on or near electrical equipment, especially computers. It's not only dangerous, but accidental spillages can also cause damage that will cost a lot to repair or replace.

81 Put music CDs and DVDs back in their cases to prevent them from getting scratched or cracked.

82 Make sure that bikes and sports equipment are properly stored and maintained to keep them safe and in good working order.

83 Favorite items of clothing will last a lot longer if they are kept clean and don't have to live in piles on the floor. A pair of expensive soccer cleats is more likely to last if properly cleaned after a muddy game.

Taking care of expensive possessions, such as bicycles, can save you money in the long run.

Q What is a warranty?

A This is a guarantee from a company that a product—such as a computer or smartphone—will work for a certain period of time. If the company is reputable, it will replace or repair the product if it stops working during the covered period. Having a warranty can give you peace of mind. Some companies also give the option to pay to extend the warranty. You must weigh the cost of this option against the money lost if something goes wrong with the product.

Sports equipment costs a lot of money. Things such as soccer cleats last longer and perform better if you take good care of them.

case study

Cell phones don't float

Archie and his friends were leaning over the side of a bridge. By the time Archie realized that his cell phone was slipping out of his top pocket, it was too late to stop it. It sank like a stone. If Archie had been a little more careful, he would not have had to spend lots of money on a new phone.

Julia's phone mysteriously disappeared one day. Ten days later, her dad saw something strange in the bottom of the toilet bowl. It was the silver tip of the antenna of Julia's cell phone. It had fallen into the toilet. Mistakes like this happen all the time when people aren't aware of their expensive possessions.

Spending and Saving Online

In addition to being a great tool for communicating with friends and researching information, the Internet is now at the forefront of retail and banking. But is it a safe and sensible place to spend and save your money?

Online banking is used by millions of people around the world. Even people who use their local banks can usually check information by accessing their accounts online. It is convenient and can be used 24/7. Online banking is a reality. You just need to make sure you are using it in the safest way.

84 Make sure your computer has full and up-to-date virus protection. This will help keep out many virus-based online banking scams, such as **Trojans**.

85 Protect yourself from criminals who want to sneak into your computer by installing a **firewall** barrier.

86 Don't be a victim of **phishing**! This type of scam sends out emails that look as though they are from real, well-known companies, or even banks. These try to trick you into giving your account numbers, passwords, or personal information by saying they need to "update your records." *Remember, no bank or reputable company will ever ask you for that kind of information in an email, or ask you to enter that type of detail at a click-through website.*

87 When your computer alerts you that there's an update or "patch" available for your operating system or your web browser, don't click "Ask me again later"! These updates and patches are the most effective tools against new scams, and they have often been created to plug the holes in an existing protective system.

Before you buy online, make sure the site you are using is safe and that the company is trustworthy.

 Q What is a computer "patch"?

 A A computer patch is like a patch used to repair a hole in a bicycle tire. When technicians realize that something in the system doesn't work, or could be easily attacked by online scams, they create a small piece of software that can be loaded to solve the problem. If you don't download and install patches, then your computer is full of holes and can leak your details.

Buying and selling online

Nothing can be more convenient or satisfying than buying or selling items online. It seems like lots of gratification for very little effort—but is it as good as it seems?

88 You may think you are getting a better deal on the Internet compared to local stores, but always remember to factor in the extras. Do you have to pay for postage and delivery? Is the payment method used secure, or will your financial details be at risk?

89 Beware of companies that pop up on the Internet offering unbelievably good deals, take your payment, and then mysteriously vanish without supplying the goods. If a price seems unbelievable, DON'T BELIEVE IT.

90 Always check the returns and repair policy before buying something online. It is easy to go into a local store and negotiate a repair or replacement for defective goods, but in the cyber world it might not be so simple.

listen up!

You need to be 18 years old or over to use the online bookseller Amazon and the auction site eBay. Other buying and selling sites have similar rules. If you want to use these sites, you will have to do so with your parents.

BE SMART

Using the Internet for savvy shopping research

The Internet is a great tool for researching products. You can compare features and prices by checking out a variety of possible retailers online. Some retailers will even let you know if the item is available in their stores and allow you to reserve one by using a special feature on their website.

Oops!

You may be very safe and responsible with your cards and PIN number, but is your identity safe online? When something is physically stolen, you usually know it has happened. When your identity is stolen online, you may never know until problems occur. So what can you do to avoid identity theft?

- Always use a password with a combination of letters and numbers that will be difficult for someone else to guess.
- Install browser security software.
- Keep your computer clean! Regularly delete your Internet search history and your temporary files, and empty your "trash."
- Use a system developed to identify any **cookies** on your computer.

What's that?

In computer language, a **cookie** is a message sent from a web server to your browser when you visit a website. The next time you visit, it knows what you looked at last time. Cookies cannot pass on viruses or access your hard drive, but they can record your usage of a website and any details you pass on to a website.

When you buy things over the telephone or online, you can never be sure where your details may end up.

Don't break the law to save money

Most of the information on the Internet is there to use for free. But some things require payment to use, or are illegal to download and share with others. Don't download things illegally—it is not worth it.

Be sure what you are doing is legal.

91 Always use a legitimate source when you buy and download music or movies. Anywhere that lets you download current music or recently released movies for free is NOT legitimate.

92 Never justify illegal file-sharing based on the fact that it saves you money. Illegal file-sharing is just as much a criminal act as if you took a DVD off a store shelf, put it in your pocket, and walked out. It is theft.

listen up!

Q What is file-sharing?

A It is the copying and sharing of digital information, such as computer data and multimedia files. Not all file-sharing is illegal. It is only illegal when it involves **copyright**-protected material.

"[Illegal file-sharing] is just so unfair to new acts trying to make it in the industry."

—Lily Allen, singer

true story

Joel Tenenbaum's big fine

In 2009 student Joel Tenenbaum was taken to court by the Recording Industry Association of America (RIAA) for illegally file-sharing 30 downloaded songs. He was convicted and fined $675,000. The fine was later reduced to $67,500, which still comes to $2,250 per song!

The RIAA has convinced U.S. courts that large fines are the best way to show people that illegal file-sharing can be a costly mistake. However, some people feel that the big music companies are just trying to protect their profits. Instead, they should be coming up with new ways of working. What do you think?

Buying DVDs from a questionable seller on the street is taking part in an illegal act. It cheats everyone who helped create the movie.

BE SMART

Illegal downloading

Recently released movies often make it on to the Internet, where they can be downloaded for free or for a small fee. This is illegal. The only way a new movie gets on the Internet is if a legitimate copy of the movie has been stolen and reproduced online, or if someone has illegally gone into a movie theater and filmed it during a performance. The sound and visual quality of a copied movie is usually very poor.

Scams and Pitfalls

When you start to look at all the problems, it seems that few things can be as dangerous or difficult as holding on to your money, or spending it safely. There are definitely scammers out there. But by being money smart and knowing what to look for, you can stay on the right track.

> **"A fool and his money are soon parted."**
>
> —Thomas Tusser, 16th-century English writer

Money scams: The same old same old

Many types of money scams have been around for hundreds of years, and only the details have changed. For example, 200 years ago, a traveling "professor" or "doctor" might have tried to sell you an anti-aging potion off the back of a horse and cart. A hundred years ago, the same useless product might have been advertised in a magazine or newspaper. Thirty years ago, you would have received junk mail, or perhaps a telephone call advertising a similar product. These days, it is more likely to turn up on the Internet. But it is the same old scam! Here are a few to look out for:

93   Avoid scams that ask you to pay in advance for products or services. They may never show up, or you may be getting and paying for more than you intended. This is the case with cell phone ringtone purchase scams. You think you are paying a one-time fee to buy ringtones, but find that you have entered into an agreement by which money is being take monthly from your bank account.

94   One major group of scams tells you that you have won a raffle or a competition and need to pay a delivery fee or tax. Some of these scams ask for personal information or your bank details to "verify" your entry. Never give this information away. It is the first step to full identity theft.

95 Beware of bogus charities! They can target you door-to-door, by letter, by telephone, or on the street. All official charities are registered and most have well-known names, either nationally or in your local area.

96 Think twice before you dial! High-cost phone calls are now the norm for phone-in competitions and computer helplines, among others. When you call one of these lines, and then wait and wait (and wait and wait) for help, you are being charged at the highest rate the whole time.

97 Watch out when using ATMs! In one scam, a device is inserted into the card slot and records the information to clone the card. Another scam uses a small camera, sometimes in a cell phone, to photograph the customer entering the PIN. Never use an ATM that looks like it has been tampered with, and always cover the keypad with your other hand when entering your PIN.

When you are using an ATM, always check carefully that no one has tampered with the machine. Look out for anything stuck onto the card slot area or in the overhang above the machine.

Q What does "buyer beware" mean?

A "Buyer beware" means it is the responsibility of a buyer or user of a service to be sure that the product he or she is getting is what was expected. If you buy a cheap, synthetic sweater, you can't expect it to be as high quality as a similar sweater made of 100 percent wool.

In most countries, consumers are protected by laws. You can return defective products or cancel contracts for goods or services within a certain period of time.

case study

Teen dream almost turns to nightmare

Have you ever dreamed of making it as a singer, actor, or model? Watch out, there are scammers out there waiting to take advantage of those dreams.

Thirteen-year-old Pippa and her friends were approached at a big fashion show by a man and woman who claimed to be scouts from a major modeling agency. They said Pippa's tall and quirky look was just what the agency wanted.

Pippa was flattered, but not stupid. She talked it over with her mom and sister. This so-called agency wanted her to pay a registration fee, plus more money for photographs and training. Pippa soon realized that, rather than being her big break, it was probably a scam. She decided not to take the offer any further.

Pippa's experience is not unique. There are many reports of teen model agency scams. Wannabe models should only approach legitimate agencies. Do research on agencies first and check with the Better Business Bureau to see if an agency has had complaints filed against it.

Oops!

Not all money scams come from outsiders trying to cheat you. Sometimes you can be your own worst enemy!

Today, more than ever, gambling is everywhere—and it can be the quickest way to lose your money! From lotteries to online poker, everyone wants to convince you to part with your money in the hope of winning big. However, there are always more losers than winners, and in some forms of gambling (such as national lotteries) the odds are millions to one against you ever winning a single penny.

Like drug addicts and alcoholics, some people become addicted to gambling. One small win makes them hope they may keep winning. The best way to stop yourself from getting caught up in such a destructive and expensive cycle is to avoid gambling altogether.

If you think you have an addiction, get help from a recognized help group such as Gamblers Anonymous.

Why Do We Need Money?

Why do we bother with money? Couldn't we get by just as well trading one thing for another? Banks, cards, cash, people out to cheat you—sometimes it all seems like too much! But it as also too late to go back now. Human beings have been using money in one form or another for at least 2,700 years.

Today, the value is not in the money itself, as it was with gold, silver, and copper coins in the past. Instead its value is set by national governments and agencies such as the World Bank and International Monetary Fund.

Metal coins have been used to pay for things since ancient times.

Oops!

Trading and bartering was fine when you could do it with people you knew in a limited area, and you could figure out the value of apples as compared to potatoes. But could we still do that now? Could you buy a computer with potatoes, or offer your skills as a doctor for apples? What if you had particularly healthy patients? You could get very hungry!

98 Find out if any local companies are quoted on the **stock market**, and follow how they are doing by looking at the stock market reports in newspapers or online. It helps you to understand how your local economy is doing and how it fits in with national and international economic trends.

What's that?

A **stock market** is a place where organized trading of company **shares** takes place. Shares are individual pieces of ownership— a "share" of the company. Each share has a value that can go up or down, depending on the popularity of the company. Many countries have a national stock market.

99 Learn more about **investment**. If buying stocks for real seems too scary, set up a fantasy stocks game between you and some friends. Start out with the same pretend amount of investment money and use it to "buy" a group of different stocks. Follow how the stocks do over a set period and see whose investments come out on top. This offers all of the fun, with none of the fear.

listen up!

Every time you buy something like a DVD or a magazine, or deposit money in your bank account, you are taking part in the international monetary system. The money you spend and save becomes part of the workings of local and national **financial institutions** that then interact with others around the globe. Like you and your friends, money doesn't stay in one place anymore. It is invested and spent all over the world.

Financing your future

After your 18th birthday, you cannot suddenly decide to take a year off to travel around the world, before starting college or getting a job. You need to plan for this first! You will need cash to finance your dreams. When your savings are making money for you through interest payments, you can start planning for future spending.

By saving up over time, you are more likely to be able to afford to live an exciting and adventurous life.

100 Don't be a money ostrich! To hide your head in the sand and pretend that money and family finances are something you don't have to worry about is immature and hard on your parents. If you talk about money issues with your family, you are less likely to run into unpleasant surprises or unreal expectations.

Q What is deferred gratification?

 A This is temporarily putting off something you really want to do or have in order to wait for something that might give you greater pleasure. Going out to buy a movie released on DVD today is instant gratification. Saving up for three years to buy a car is deferred gratification.

 **case study**

Daniel wanted to learn to fly a plane practically from the moment he knew what a plane was. Before he was 10 years old, he was already saving up for flying lessons. He always asked for cash for birthdays and Hanukkah, and he got a Saturday job as soon as he was able, with most of his cash going into the flying fund.

When he finally started flying lessons, they lived up to his expectations. Dan did his solo flight and got his pilot's license before learning to drive! He is now at college studying aeronautic engineering, and he's still flying.

listen up!

Money is not great in itself. It is just a way to buy stuff. You need some of that stuff to survive, such as food, clothing, and shelter. Other things make your life nicer or make you more comfortable. But wealth is not the answer to all of life's problems. Money will not tell you how to make good friends, or what music to like, or what subject to study in college. Large amounts of money can sometimes even make your life more difficult, with more responsibilities and more challenging choices.

101 Always see money and wealth in perspective. Understand what money can and can't do. As the old saying goes, "Money can't buy you happiness."

Glossary

accountant someone who is professionally trained to deal with the finances of organizations and individuals

carbon footprint total emissions of greenhouse gases caused by an activity or the production of a product. A person's carbon footprint is the sum of all of the greenhouse-gas-creating activities that he or she caused to occur over a given period of time.

clone term used by banks to describe credit or debit cards that have had their details copied and used illegally

cookie message sent from a web server to a person's web browser identifying information a person is using or entering on to a website

copyright law that protects the right to use and the ownership of musical, artistic, and literary works. Copyright law gives the creator of a work the exclusive ownership of his or her creation for a set period of time.

counterfeit make an exact imitation of something, such as money, in order to deceive people

credit history record of all borrowings and repayments made by a person

credit union financial institution controlled and owned by its members

entrepreneur someone who starts or organizes a business, usually taking a financial risk

ethical goods that are produced and sold in ways that are fair to the people who have worked on them

financial institution organization such as a bank or credit union

financial literacy understanding of money and finances

firewall system installed in a personal computer or a computer network to block unauthorized access, but to allow authorized access

fraudulent usage illegal use of something with an intention to deceive

impulse buying purchasing an item without much care or thought. Impulse buys are often not needed or are a poor value for the money spent.

interest amount of money paid on savings or charged on borrowings or debt. The interest rate is the percentage paid or charged.

investment using money to make a profit

logo symbol used by a company to identify a product as belonging to its brand. It is usually a small shape, word, or series of letters.

mortgage loan taken out to buy property

peer pressure pressure from your friends or others in a similar age group to influence how you act or what you think

phishing email scam in which the scammer tries to get information from you by making you think you are dealing with a real, legitimate company. Some forms of phishing are also known as "spoofing."

résumé brief report of a person's education and work experience, as well as certain biographical details. It is usually used to support an application for a job, or for education or training.

share small unit of ownership of a company

stock market place where shares are bought and sold. Some countries have national stock markets.

Trojan computer program that seems to be useful but is designed to be harmful. Trojans can destroy information on your computer.

Find Out More

Books

Ash, Rebecca. *The Spend Less Handbook: 365 Tips for a Better Quality of Life While Actually Spending Less*. Hoboken, N.J.: Wiley, 2008.

Blatt, Jessica. *Money: Getting Smart About Making It, Saving It, and Spending It*. New York: Watson-Guptill, 2008.

Hall, Alvin. *Show Me the Money*. New York: Dorling Kindersley, 2008.

Hollander, Barbara. *Life Skills: Managing Money*. Chicago: Heinemann Library, 2009.

Hollander, Barbara. *Life Skills: Raising Money*. Chicago: Heinemann Library, 2009.

Websites

www.fdic.gov/consumers/consumer/news/cnsum06/index.html

This website of the Federal Deposit Insurance Corporation (FDIC) is full of useful advice for teens about managing money.

www.mymoney.gov

This U.S. government website is full of advice about how to manage money, including useful tools such as budgeting worksheets.

www.atg.wa.gov/teenconsumer/index.htm

This "Teen Consumer Scrapbook" is full of information about all aspects of money and how it relates to young people.

www.ftc.gov/gettingcredit/

This website of the Federal Trade Commission (FTC) gives advice about getting credit and keeping a good credit history. It includes advice about scams such as identity theft.

www.ftc.gov/bcp/edu/microsites/youarehere/site.html#/security-plaza

This interactive FTC website teaches teens how to protect their privacy, both online and offline.

www.ethicalshopping.com

This website has lots of information about ethical shopping.

Topics to research

- Can using the Internet help you save money? Research an item you are interested in buying using brand websites and price comparison websites. Figure out how you can get the best bargains. Remember to be careful if you are considering buying online.

- Does budgeting save you money? Try making yourself a budget for a week or a month. Figure out which expenditures are the most important. If you can, factor earning and saving into your budget.

- Find out more about music copyright law and the problem of illegal downloading. Are you and your friends getting your music legally? What are governments and the music industry doing to tackle the problem of illegal downloads and file sharing?

- Play a "fantasy" stock market game with your friends or classmates. Each of you could begin with the same budget and then research

  the best stocks to "buy" and when to "sell." See who comes out on top after a few months as a fantasy investor.

Index